LEAN AND CLEAN: LOW FAT RECIPES FOR A HEALTHIER YOU

First edition. March 19, 2024.

Copyright © 2024 Brintalos Georgios.

ISBN: 979-8224565078

Written by Brintalos Georgios.

Table of Contents

Lean And Clean: Low Fat Recipes For A Healthier You

Turkey and bean chili

Ingredients:

- 1 lb ground turkey
- 1 can kidney beans
- 1 can diced tomatoes
- 1 onion, chopped
- 1 bell pepper, diced
- 2 cloves garlic, minced
- 1 tbsp chili powder
- 1 tsp cumin
- 1/2 tsp salt

Equipment:

1. Dutch oven
2. Wooden spoon
3. Chef's knife
4. Cutting board
5. Pot
6. Ladle

Methods:

Step 1: In a large pot, heat olive oil over medium-high heat.

Step 2: Add diced onions and cook until softened.

Step 3: Stir in ground turkey and cook until browned.

Step 4: Mix in chili powder, cumin, and garlic powder.

Step 5: Add chopped bell peppers, diced tomatoes, and kidney beans.

Step 6: Pour in chicken broth and bring to a simmer.

Step 7: Let simmer for 30 minutes, stirring occasionally.

Step 8: Season with salt and pepper to taste.

Step 9: Serve hot with your favorite toppings such as shredded cheese, sour cream, and cilantro.

Step 10: Enjoy your delicious turkey and bean chili!

Helpful Tips:

BRINTALOS GEORGIOS

1. Start by browning ground turkey in a large pot before adding diced onions, garlic, and bell peppers for flavor.

2. Season with chili powder, cumin, paprika, and a pinch of cayenne for a spicy kick.

3. Add drained and rinsed beans (like kidney or black beans) along with diced tomatoes and broth.

4. Let the chili simmer for at least 30 minutes to allow the flavors to meld together.

5. Serve hot with toppings like shredded cheese, sour cream, and diced avocado for a delicious meal. Enjoy!

Veggie kabobs with hummus

Ingredients:

- 2 zucchinis
- 1 large bell pepper
- 1 red onion
- 1 cup cherry tomatoes
- 1/4 cup olive oil
- 1 tsp garlic powder
- 1 tsp paprika
- 1/2 tsp salt
- 4 wooden skewers
- 1 cup hummus

Equipment:

1. Knife
2. Cutting board
3. Skewers
4. Grill pan
5. Mixing bowl

Methods:

Step 1: Soak wooden skewers in water for at least 30 minutes.

Step 2: Preheat grill to medium-high heat.

Step 3: Cut up vegetables of your choice into bite-sized pieces.

Step 4: Thread vegetables onto the skewers, alternating between each type.

Step 5: Brush kabobs with olive oil and season with salt and pepper.

Step 6: Grill kabobs for about 10-12 minutes, turning occasionally, until vegetables are cooked and slightly charred.

Step 7: Serve veggie kabobs with hummus for dipping.

Step 8: Enjoy your delicious and healthy meal!

Helpful Tips:

1. Soak wooden skewers in water for at least 30 minutes to prevent burning.
2. Cut vegetables into evenly-sized pieces for even cooking.

3. Marinate the vegetables in a mixture of olive oil, lemon juice, garlic, and your favorite herbs for added flavor.

4. Don't overcrowd the skewers to ensure even grilling.

5. Grill the kabobs on medium-high heat for about 10-15 minutes, turning occasionally.

6. Serve the veggie kabobs with a side of creamy hummus for dipping.

7. Enjoy your flavorful and healthy meal!

Baked sweet potato fries

Ingredients:
- 2 sweet potatoes
- 2 tbsp olive oil
- 1 tsp paprika
- 1/2 tsp garlic powder
- Salt and pepper to taste

Equipment:
1. Baking sheet
2. Knife
3. Cutting board
4. Mixing bowl
5. Spatula

Methods:
Step 1: Preheat the oven to 400°F.

Step 2: Wash and peel sweet potatoes.

Step 3: Cut sweet potatoes into thin fries.

Step 4: In a large bowl, toss sweet potato fries with olive oil, salt, pepper, and any desired seasonings.

Step 5: Spread fries in a single layer on a baking sheet lined with parchment paper.

Step 6: Bake for 20-30 minutes, flipping halfway through, until fries are crispy and golden brown.

Step 7: Remove from oven and let cool slightly before serving.

Step 8: Enjoy your delicious baked sweet potato fries as a healthy snack or side dish.

Helpful Tips:
1. Cut sweet potatoes into uniform strips for even cooking.

2. Soak the sweet potato strips in cold water for at least 30 minutes to remove excess starch.

3. Preheat your oven to at least 400°F (200°C) to ensure crispy fries.

4. Toss the sweet potato strips in olive oil and your choice of seasonings before baking.

5. Arrange the fries in a single layer on a baking sheet to prevent them from steaming.

6. Flip the fries halfway through baking for even crispiness.

7. Serve hot and enjoy with your favorite dipping sauce.

Chicken and vegetable stir-fry

Ingredients:

- 1 lb chicken breast, thinly sliced
- 1 red bell pepper, sliced
- 1 cup broccoli florets
- 1/2 cup sliced carrots
- 1/4 cup soy sauce
- 2 tbsp vegetable oil

Equipment:

1. Wok
2. Spatula
3. Knife
4. Cutting board
5. Mixing bowl

Methods:

Step 1: Heat a wok or large skillet over high heat.

Step 2: Add 1 tablespoon of vegetable oil to the pan and swirl to coat.

Step 3: Add 1 pound of diced chicken breast and stir-fry until cooked through.

Step 4: Remove the chicken from the pan and set aside.

Step 5: Add another tablespoon of oil to the pan and stir-fry 2 cups of mixed vegetables (such as bell peppers, broccoli, and carrots) until tender-crisp.

Step 6: Return the chicken to the pan and add a sauce made from a mixture of soy sauce, ginger, garlic, and brown sugar.

Step 7: Stir-fry for an additional 2-3 minutes until everything is heated through.

Step 8: Serve hot over steamed rice. Enjoy!

Helpful Tips:

1. Prep all ingredients beforehand: chop vegetables, slice chicken, and mix sauce.

2. Use a wok or large skillet for even cooking.

3. Cook chicken first until no longer pink, then set aside.

4. Stir-fry vegetables in the same pan, starting with longer cooking veggies like carrots and ending with quick-cooking ones like spinach.

5. Add chicken back to the pan and pour sauce over everything, stirring well.

6. Cook until sauce thickens and everything is heated through.

7. Serve over rice or noodles for a complete meal. Enjoy your delicious chicken and vegetable stir-fry!

Grilled swordfish

Ingredients:

- 4 swordfish steaks (6 oz each)
- 2 tbsp olive oil
- 2 tbsp lemon juice
- 2 cloves garlic, minced
- Salt and pepper to taste

Equipment:

1. Grill
2. Tongs
3. Basting Brush
4. Fish Spatula
5. Marinade Bowl
6. Plate for Serving

Methods:

Step 1: Preheat the grill to medium-high heat.

Step 2: Brush the swordfish steaks with olive oil and season with salt and pepper.

Step 3: Place the swordfish steaks on the grill and cook for 4-5 minutes on each side, or until the fish is opaque and flakes easily with a fork.

Step 4: Remove the swordfish from the grill and let it rest for a few minutes before serving.

Step 5: Serve the grilled swordfish with your favorite side dishes and enjoy!

Helpful Tips:

1. Marinate the swordfish in a mixture of olive oil, lemon juice, garlic, and herbs for at least 30 minutes before grilling.

2. Preheat the grill to high heat and oil the grates to prevent sticking.

3. Grill the swordfish for about 4-5 minutes per side, or until it easily flakes with a fork.

4. Avoid overcooking the swordfish, as it can become dry and tough.

5. Serve the grilled swordfish with a side of lemon wedges and fresh herbs for a burst of flavor. Enjoy!

Cucumber and tomato salad

Ingredients:

- 2 cucumbers, sliced
- 4 tomatoes, diced
- 1/4 red onion, thinly sliced
- 1/4 cup fresh parsley
- 2 tbsp olive oil
- Salt and pepper to taste

Equipment:

1. Knife
2. Cutting board
3. Mixing bowl
4. Salad tongs
5. Vegetable peeler

Methods:

Step 1: Start by washing and slicing 2 medium cucumbers and 3 medium tomatoes.

Step 2: In a large bowl, combine the sliced cucumbers and tomatoes.

Step 3: Add ¼ cup of chopped red onion and ¼ cup of chopped fresh parsley to the bowl.

Step 4: In a small bowl, whisk together 3 tablespoons of olive oil, 2 tablespoons of red wine vinegar, 1 teaspoon of honey, and a pinch of salt and pepper.

Step 5: Pour the dressing over the cucumber and tomato mixture and toss to combine.

Step 6: Let the salad sit for at least 10 minutes to allow the flavors to meld together.

Step 7: Serve and enjoy!

Helpful Tips:

1. Start by slicing cucumbers and tomatoes into evenly sized pieces for a uniform texture.

2. Season with salt and pepper to taste, and add some fresh herbs like parsley or dill for extra flavor.

3. Drizzle with a simple dressing of olive oil, lemon juice or vinegar, and a dash of honey for sweetness.

4. Let the salad sit for at least 15 minutes to allow the flavors to meld together before serving.

5. Consider adding some diced red onion or crumbled feta cheese for added depth of flavor.

6. Serve chilled for a refreshing and healthy side dish.

Broccoli and chicken casserole

Ingredients:

- 2 cups cooked chicken
- 2 cups broccoli florets
- 1 cup shredded cheddar cheese
- 1 can cream of chicken soup

Equipment:

1. Knife
2. Cutting board
3. Saucepan
4. Wooden spoon
5. Baking dish
6. Oven rack

Methods:

Step 1: Preheat the oven to 375°F and grease a casserole dish.

Step 2: In a skillet, cook 1 pound of diced chicken until browned.

Step 3: In a pot of boiling water, blanch 1 head of chopped broccoli for 2 minutes.

Step 4: In a bowl, mix together 1 can of cream of chicken soup, 1 cup of shredded cheddar cheese, and 1/2 cup of milk.

Step 5: Layer the cooked chicken and broccoli in the casserole dish.

Step 6: Pour the cheese mixture over the chicken and broccoli.

Step 7: Bake in the oven for 25-30 minutes or until bubbly and golden brown. Enjoy!

Helpful Tips:

1. Start by preheating your oven to 375°F.

2. Cut broccoli into florets and cut chicken into bite-sized pieces.

3. In a large skillet, cook chicken with olive oil until browned.

4. In a separate bowl, mix together cooked chicken, broccoli, cream of chicken soup, milk, and shredded cheese.

5. Transfer the mixture into a casserole dish and top with breadcrumbs.

6. Bake for 25-30 minutes or until bubbly and breadcrumbs are golden brown.

7. Let it cool for a few minutes before serving.

8. Enjoy your delicious and nutritious broccoli and chicken casserole!

Asian cabbage slaw with chicken

Ingredients:
- 1/2 head cabbage
- 1 carrot
- 1/2 red onion
- 1/4 cup soy sauce
- 2 tbsp rice vinegar
- 1 tsp sesame oil
- 1/2 tsp ginger
- 1/2 lb cooked chicken

Equipment:
1. Knife
2. Cutting board
3. Mixing bowl
4. Skillet
5. Tongs

Methods:
Step 1: Begin by shredding a head of cabbage and chopping up some green onions.

Step 2: Next, cook some chicken breast until fully cooked and then shred into smaller pieces.

Step 3: In a large bowl, combine the cabbage, green onions, and shredded chicken.

Step 4: In a separate bowl, mix together soy sauce, sesame oil, rice vinegar, and a dash of honey to create a dressing.

Step 5: Pour the dressing over the cabbage mixture and toss until everything is evenly coated.

Step 6: Let the slaw sit in the fridge for at least 30 minutes before serving.

Step 7: Enjoy your delicious Asian cabbage slaw with chicken!

Helpful Tips:

BRINTALOS GEORGIOS

1. Start by shredding Napa cabbage, carrots, and bell peppers for your slaw base.

2. Marinate chicken in a mixture of soy sauce, sesame oil, ginger, and garlic before grilling or pan-frying.

3. Toss the slaw veggies with a dressing made from rice vinegar, soy sauce, honey, and lime juice.

4. Mix in some chopped cilantro and sliced green onions for added flavor.

5. Top the slaw with the sliced cooked chicken.

6. For extra crunch, sprinkle toasted sesame seeds or crushed peanuts on top.

7. Serve the Asian cabbage slaw with chicken as a delicious and healthy meal option.

Cod and vegetable foil packets

Ingredients:
- 4 cod fillets
- 2 zucchinis, sliced
- 1 red bell pepper, sliced
- 1 red onion, sliced
- 4 tbsp olive oil
- 4 garlic cloves, minced
- Salt and pepper to taste

Equipment:
1. Baking sheet
2. Aluminum foil
3. Knife
4. Cutting board
5. Mixing bowl

Methods:
Step 1: Preheat the oven to 400°F.

Step 2: Cut 4 pieces of aluminum foil into squares.

Step 3: Place a cod fillet in the center of each foil square.

Step 4: Season cod with salt, pepper, and olive oil.

Step 5: Add your favorite vegetables like bell peppers, zucchini, and cherry tomatoes on top of the cod.

Step 6: Fold the foil over the cod and vegetables to create a packet.

Step 7: Place the foil packets on a baking sheet and bake in the oven for 15-20 minutes, or until the cod is cooked through.

Step 8: Carefully open the packets and serve the cod and vegetables hot. Enjoy!

Helpful Tips:
1. Start by preheating the oven to 400°F.

2. Cut the cod into individual portions and place each piece onto a sheet of aluminum foil.

3. Add your choice of chopped vegetables such as bell peppers, onions, and zucchini on top of the fish.

4. Drizzle with olive oil and season with salt, pepper, and herbs like dill or parsley.

5. Fold the foil over the fish and vegetables to create a sealed packet.

6. Bake in the oven for 15-20 minutes or until the fish is cooked through and the vegetables are tender.

7. Carefully open the foil packets to serve and enjoy a delicious and healthy meal.

Turkey and black bean soup

Ingredients:

- 1 lb ground turkey
- 1 onion, diced
- 2 cans black beans
- 1 can diced tomatoes
- 4 cups chicken broth
- 1 tsp cumin
- Salt and pepper to taste

Equipment:

1. Large soup pot
2. Wooden spoon
3. Ladle
4. Knife
5. Cutting board

Methods:

Step 1: In a large pot, heat olive oil over medium heat.

Step 2: Add chopped onions and garlic, and sauté until soft.

Step 3: Stir in diced turkey breast and cook until browned.

Step 4: Add in black beans, diced tomatoes, chicken broth, and spices.

Step 5: Bring soup to a boil, then reduce heat and let simmer for 20-25 minutes.

Step 6: Taste and adjust seasoning as needed.

Step 7: Serve hot, garnished with fresh cilantro and a squeeze of lime juice.

Step 8: Enjoy your delicious and hearty Turkey and Black Bean Soup!

Helpful Tips:

1. Start by sautéing onions, garlic, and celery in olive oil for added flavor.

2. Use a flavorful broth, such as chicken or vegetable, for the base of the soup.

3. Add seasonings like cumin, chili powder, and paprika for a delicious kick.

4. Consider using leftover Thanksgiving turkey for added protein and flavor.

5. Simmer the soup low and slow to allow the flavors to blend together.

6. Serve the soup with a dollop of sour cream and a sprinkle of fresh cilantro for a tasty finish.

Chickpea and vegetable curry

Ingredients:

- 2 cans of chickpeas
- 1 onion, diced
- 2 bell peppers, sliced
- 1 cup of coconut milk
- 2 tbsp curry powder
- Salt and pepper to taste

Equipment:

1. Cutting board
2. Chef's knife
3. Saute pan
4. Wooden spoon
5. Pot
6. Ladle

Methods:

Step 1: Heat oil in a large pot over medium heat.

Step 2: Add diced onions and garlic, and sauté until onions are translucent.

Step 3: Stir in curry powder, cumin, and turmeric, and cook for 1 minute.

Step 4: Add diced tomatoes, chickpeas, and vegetable broth to the pot.

Step 5: Bring mixture to a simmer and cook for 15 minutes, stirring occasionally.

Step 6: Add chopped vegetables of your choice (such as bell peppers, zucchini, and carrots) to the pot.

Step 7: Cook for an additional 10 minutes, or until vegetables are tender.

Step 8: Serve hot over rice or with naan bread. Enjoy your chickpea and vegetable curry!

Helpful Tips:

1. Start by sautéing onions, ginger, and garlic in oil until fragrant.

2. Add your favorite curry spices like turmeric, cumin, and coriander for flavor.

3. Stir in chopped vegetables like bell peppers, carrots, and tomatoes for added nutrition.

4. Pour in vegetable broth and cooked chickpeas, simmer until vegetables are tender.

5. Finish with a splash of coconut milk and fresh cilantro for a creamy finish.

6. Serve over rice or with naan for a satisfying meal. Enjoy!

Grilled tofu and vegetable skewers

Ingredients:
- 1 block tofu, cubed
- 1 zucchini, sliced
- 1 bell pepper, diced
- 1 red onion, quartered
- 1/4 cup soy sauce
- 2 tbsp olive oil
- 2 cloves garlic, minced

Equipment:
1. Skewers
2. Grill pan
3. Tongs
4. Basting brush
5. Cutting board
6. Knife

Methods:

Step 1: Soak wooden skewers in water for at least 30 minutes to prevent them from burning on the grill.

Step 2: Cut tofu into cubes and prepare vegetables like bell peppers, zucchini, and cherry tomatoes.

Step 3: Thread the tofu and vegetables onto the skewers, alternating between each ingredient.

Step 4: Mix together a marinade using soy sauce, garlic, ginger, and olive oil.

Step 5: Brush the skewers with the marinade and let them sit for at least 15 minutes.

Step 6: Preheat the grill to medium-high heat and place the skewers on the grill.

Step 7: Grill for about 10-15 minutes, turning occasionally, until vegetables are tender and tofu is lightly browned.

Step 8: Serve hot and enjoy your delicious grilled tofu and vegetable skewers!

Helpful Tips:

1. Marinate tofu in a flavorful sauce for at least 30 minutes before grilling to enhance the taste.

2. Alternate tofu cubes with vegetables like bell peppers, zucchini, and cherry tomatoes on skewers for a colorful presentation.

3. Brush the skewers with oil before grilling to prevent sticking and help achieve those beautiful grill marks.

4. Preheat the grill to medium-high heat and grill skewers for about 8-10 minutes, turning occasionally, until tofu is golden and vegetables are tender.

5. Serve with a side of rice or quinoa and a drizzle of lemon juice or a sprinkle of fresh herbs for added flavor.

Shrimp and avocado salad

Ingredients:
- 1 lb shrimp
- 2 avocados
- 1 red onion
- 1 lime
- 1/4 cup cilantro
- Salt and pepper to taste

Equipment:
1. Knife
2. Cutting board
3. Mixing bowl
4. Whisk
5. Serving spoon

Methods:
Step 1: In a medium-sized bowl, mix together 1 pound of cooked and diced shrimp and 1 diced avocado.

Step 2: Add in 1/4 cup of diced red onion and 1/4 cup of chopped cilantro.

Step 3: In a separate small bowl, whisk together 2 tablespoons of olive oil, the juice of 1 lime, and salt and pepper to taste.

Step 4: Pour the dressing over the shrimp and avocado mixture and gently toss to combine.

Step 5: Serve the salad on a bed of mixed greens or in lettuce cups for a low-carb option.

Step 6: Enjoy your fresh and delicious shrimp and avocado salad!

Helpful Tips:
1. Start by marinating the shrimp in a combination of olive oil, garlic, lemon juice, salt, and pepper for added flavor.

2. Use ripe avocados that are slightly firm to the touch for the best texture in the salad.

3. Cook the shrimp just until they turn opaque and pink, being careful not to overcook them to prevent them from becoming rubbery.

4. Toss the shrimp and avocado with a mixture of greens, cherry tomatoes, red onion, and a light dressing for a well-balanced salad.

5. Consider adding additional toppings such as crumbled feta cheese or toasted nuts for added texture and flavor. Enjoy!

Cauliflower rice with shrimp

Ingredients:
- 1 head cauliflower
- 1 lb shrimp
- 1 onion
- 2 cloves garlic
- 1 red bell pepper
- 1 tsp cumin
- 1/2 tsp paprika
- salt and pepper to taste

Equipment:
1. Knife
2. Cutting board
3. Skillet
4. Spatula
5. Strainer
6. Mixing bowl

Methods:
Step 1: Start by heating a tablespoon of olive oil in a large skillet over medium heat.

Step 2: Add diced onion and minced garlic to the skillet and sauté until fragrant.

Step 3: Stir in chopped cauliflower and cook for about 5-7 minutes, until cauliflower is tender.

Step 4: Push the cauliflower to one side of the skillet and add the shrimp to the empty space.

Step 5: Cook the shrimp for 2-3 minutes on each side, until pink and cooked through.

Step 6: Mix the shrimp with the cauliflower rice and season with salt, pepper, and any desired herbs or spices.

Step 7: Serve hot and enjoy your delicious cauliflower rice with shrimp.

Helpful Tips:

1. Start by thoroughly washing and drying the cauliflower before cutting into florets.

2. Use a food processor to pulse the cauliflower florets until they resemble rice grains.

3. Heat a skillet over medium heat and add a little oil before cooking the cauliflower rice for about 5-7 minutes.

4. Season the cauliflower rice with salt, pepper, and any other preferred spices or herbs.

5. In a separate pan, cook shrimp until they turn pink and are fully cooked.

6. Mix the cooked shrimp into the cauliflower rice and serve hot.

7. Garnish with fresh herbs or a squeeze of lemon juice for extra flavor.

Sauteed spinach with garlic

Ingredients:
- 1 lb fresh spinach
- 2 cloves garlic
- 2 tbsp olive oil
- Salt and pepper to taste

Equipment:
1. Skillet
2. Wooden spoon
3. Chef's knife
4. Cutting board
5. Tongs

Methods:
Step 1: Heat a pan over medium heat and add a tablespoon of olive oil.

Step 2: Add 2 minced garlic cloves and saute for 1-2 minutes until fragrant.

Step 3: Add 4 cups of fresh spinach to the pan and toss to coat in the garlic oil.

Step 4: Cook the spinach for 3-4 minutes, stirring occasionally, until wilted.

Step 5: Season with salt and pepper to taste.

Step 6: Remove from heat and serve hot as a side dish or a topping for protein.

Step 7: Enjoy your delicious sauteed spinach with garlic!

Helpful Tips:
1. Heat a large skillet over medium heat and add olive oil.

2. Add minced garlic to the skillet and sauté until fragrant.

3. Add fresh spinach leaves to the skillet and toss until wilted.

4. Season with salt, pepper, and a pinch of red pepper flakes for added flavor.

5. Do not overcook the spinach as it can become mushy.

6. Serve immediately as a side dish or as a bed for grilled chicken or fish.

7. Garnish with a squeeze of fresh lemon juice for a pop of brightness.

8. Enjoy this healthy and flavorful dish!

Baked turkey meatloaf

Ingredients:

- 1 lb ground turkey
- 1/2 cup breadcrumbs
- 1/4 cup ketchup
- 1 egg
- 1/4 cup diced onion
- 1/4 cup diced bell pepper
- 1/2 tsp salt
- 1/4 tsp pepper

Equipment:

1. Mixing bowl
2. Whisk
3. Baking dish
4. Meat thermometer
5. Oven mitts

Methods:

Step 1: Preheat the oven to 375°F and line a baking sheet with foil.

Step 2: In a large bowl, mix together ground turkey, breadcrumbs, diced onions, minced garlic, ketchup, Worcestershire sauce, salt, and pepper.

Step 3: Shape the turkey mixture into a loaf shape and place it on the prepared baking sheet.

Step 4: In a small bowl, whisk together ketchup, brown sugar, and mustard to make a glaze.

Step 5: Brush the glaze over the meatloaf.

Step 6: Bake the turkey meatloaf in the preheated oven for 45-50 minutes or until fully cooked through.

Step 7: Let the meatloaf rest for 5 minutes before slicing and serving. Enjoy!

Helpful Tips:

BRINTALOS GEORGIOS

1. Preheat your oven to 350°F before starting to prepare your turkey meatloaf.

2. Use lean ground turkey to reduce excess fat and prevent your meatloaf from becoming greasy.

3. Incorporate flavorful ingredients such as sautéed onions, garlic, and herbs for added taste.

4. Mix in breadcrumbs or oats as a binder to hold the meatloaf together.

5. Shape the meatloaf into a loaf shape on a baking sheet lined with parchment paper to prevent sticking.

6. Brush the top of the meatloaf with a glaze made from ketchup, brown sugar, and mustard for a tasty, caramelized finish.

7. Bake the turkey meatloaf for approximately 1 hour, or until it reaches an internal temperature of 165°F.

8. Allow the meatloaf to rest for 10 minutes before slicing and serving. Enjoy!

Grilled salmon Caesar salad

Ingredients:
- 1 lb salmon fillets
- 1 head romaine lettuce
- 1/2 cup Caesar dressing
- 1/3 cup shredded Parmesan cheese

Equipment:
1. Grill
2. Mixing bowl
3. Salad tongs
4. Salad spinner
5. Whisk

Methods:
Step 1: Preheat the grill to medium-high heat.

Step 2: Season the salmon fillets with salt, pepper, and olive oil.

Step 3: Grill the salmon fillets for 4-5 minutes per side, or until they are opaque and flaky.

Step 4: In a large bowl, toss together romaine lettuce, croutons, and Caesar dressing.

Step 5: Divide the salad onto plates.

Step 6: Top each salad with a grilled salmon fillet.

Step 7: Garnish with Parmesan cheese and lemon wedges.

Step 8: Serve immediately and enjoy your delicious Grilled Salmon Caesar Salad!

Helpful Tips:
1. Preheat your grill to medium heat to cook the salmon evenly.

2. Season the salmon with salt, pepper, and a squeeze of lemon juice before grilling.

3. Grill the salmon for about 4-5 minutes per side, or until it flakes easily with a fork.

4. Use a store-bought Caesar dressing or make your own with ingredients like anchovies, garlic, Dijon mustard, and Parmesan cheese.

5. Toss romaine lettuce with the Caesar dressing and top with croutons, shaved Parmesan, and grilled salmon for a delicious and satisfying salad.

Chicken and quinoa bowl

Ingredients:

- 1 cup quinoa
- 2 cups water
- 1 lb boneless, skinless chicken breasts
- 1 tbsp olive oil
- 1 tsp garlic powder
- 1 tsp cumin
- Salt and pepper to taste
- 1 avocado, sliced

Equipment:

1. Cutting board
2. Knife
3. Saucepan
4. Mixing bowl
5. Whisk
6. Tongs

Methods:

Step 1: Rinse 1 cup of quinoa thoroughly and cook according to package instructions.

Step 2: Season 2 boneless, skinless chicken breasts with salt, pepper, and any desired seasoning.

Step 3: Heat a grill pan over medium-high heat and cook chicken for 6-8 minutes per side or until cooked through.

Step 4: Let chicken rest for 5 minutes, then slice into strips.

Step 5: In a bowl, combine cooked quinoa, chicken slices, and your choice of veggies (such as cherry tomatoes, cucumber, and avocado).

Step 6: Drizzle with a dressing of your choice and enjoy your healthy chicken and quinoa bowl!

Helpful Tips:

BRINTALOS GEORGIOS

1. Start by marinating the chicken in olive oil, lemon juice, and your favorite seasonings for added flavor.

2. Cook the quinoa in chicken broth instead of water for a richer taste.

3. Sear the chicken on high heat to get a crispy exterior while keeping it juicy on the inside.

4. Don't overcook the quinoa - fluff it with a fork and let it rest for a few minutes before serving.

5. Add fresh veggies like cucumbers, tomatoes, and avocado for a nutritious and colorful topping.

6. Drizzle with a homemade tzatziki or tahini sauce for a Mediterranean flair.

Bean and vegetable burritos

Ingredients:
- 1 can of black beans
- 1 cup of diced tomatoes
- 1/2 cup of diced red onion
- 1 cup of shredded cheddar cheese
- 4 large whole wheat tortillas

Equipment:
1. Knife
2. Cutting board
3. Pan
4. Spatula
5. Mixing bowl

Methods:
Step 1: Heat a tablespoon of olive oil in a skillet over medium heat.

Step 2: Add diced onions, bell peppers, and garlic to the skillet and sauté until softened.

Step 3: Stir in a can of black beans, chili powder, cumin, and salt. Cook for another 5 minutes.

Step 4: Warm the tortillas in a separate skillet or in the microwave.

Step 5: Spoon the bean and vegetable mixture onto each tortilla.

Step 6: Top with shredded cheese, diced tomatoes, avocado slices, and a dollop of sour cream.

Step 7: Roll up the burritos and serve hot. Enjoy your delicious bean and vegetable burritos!

Helpful Tips:
1. Start by sautéing diced onions and garlic in olive oil for extra flavor.

2. Cook your beans (such as black beans or pinto beans) until they are soft and well-seasoned with spices like cumin and chili powder.

3. Add chopped bell peppers, corn, and diced tomatoes to the bean mixture for added texture and flavor.

4. Warm your tortillas before assembling the burritos to make them more pliable and easier to roll.

5. Top your burritos with salsa, avocado slices, and a sprinkle of shredded cheese for a delicious finishing touch. Enjoy!

Grilled vegetable pasta salad

Ingredients:

- 2 zucchinis
- 1 red bell pepper
- 1 yellow bell pepper
- 1 red onion
- 1 cup cherry tomatoes
- 8 oz pasta
- 1/4 cup olive oil
- 2 tbsp balsamic vinegar
- Salt and pepper to taste

Equipment:

1. Mixing bowl
2. Wooden spoon
3. Chef's knife
4. Cutting board
5. Grilling pan

Methods:

Step 1: Preheat the grill to medium-high heat.

Step 2: Toss chopped vegetables (bell peppers, zucchini, cherry tomatoes) with olive oil, salt, and pepper.

Step 3: Place vegetables on grill and cook until lightly charred and tender, about 8-10 minutes.

Step 4: Cook pasta according to package instructions until al dente, then rinse with cold water and drain.

Step 5: In a large bowl, toss the grilled vegetables with the cooked pasta.

Step 6: Add in chopped fresh herbs (parsley, basil), crumbled feta cheese, and a drizzle of balsamic vinaigrette.

Step 7: Serve chilled or at room temperature. Enjoy!

Helpful Tips:

BRINTALOS GEORGIOS

1. Start by grilling a variety of colorful vegetables, such as bell peppers, zucchini, and cherry tomatoes, for added flavor and nutrition.

2. Cook the pasta just until al dente to prevent it from becoming mushy in the salad.

3. Be generous with fresh herbs, such as basil and parsley, to add brightness and freshness to the dish.

4. Toss the grilled vegetables and pasta with a simple vinaigrette made from olive oil, balsamic vinegar, and Dijon mustard for a flavorful dressing.

5. Finish the salad with a sprinkle of crumbled feta or grated Parmesan cheese for a touch of creaminess and saltiness.

Turkey and spinach meatballs

Ingredients:
- 500g ground turkey
- 2 cups fresh spinach, chopped
- 1/2 cup breadcrumbs
- 1/4 cup grated Parmesan cheese

Equipment:
1. Mixing bowl
2. Wooden spoon
3. Skillet
4. Measuring cups
5. Knife
6. Cutting board

Methods:
Step 1: Preheat the oven to 375°F and line a baking sheet with parchment paper.

Step 2: In a large bowl, mix together ground turkey, chopped spinach, breadcrumbs, egg, minced garlic, grated parmesan cheese, salt, and pepper.

Step 3: Shape the mixture into meatballs and place them on the prepared baking sheet.

Step 4: Bake the meatballs in the preheated oven for 20-25 minutes, or until cooked through.

Step 5: Serve the turkey and spinach meatballs hot with your favorite sauce or pasta.

Step 6: Enjoy your delicious and nutritious meal!

Helpful Tips:
1. Use lean ground turkey to reduce fat content in the meatballs.

2. Thaw frozen spinach and squeeze out excess water before mixing with the turkey.

3. Add grated Parmesan cheese for extra flavor and moisture.

4. Season with garlic, onion powder, salt, and pepper for a savory taste.

5. For better binding, mix in breadcrumbs or a beaten egg with the meat mixture.

6. Shape into evenly sized meatballs for even cooking.

7. Bake in the oven at 400°F for 15-20 minutes or until cooked through.

8. Serve with marinara sauce or Greek yogurt for dipping. Enjoy!

Teriyaki tofu stir-fry

Ingredients:
- 1 block of tofu, cubed
- 1/4 cup of teriyaki sauce
- 1 bell pepper, sliced
- 1 onion, sliced

Equipment:
1. Wok
2. Spatula
3. Knife
4. Cutting board
5. Tongs

Methods:
Step 1: Cut tofu into cubes and marinate in teriyaki sauce for at least 30 minutes.

Step 2: Heat oil in a skillet over medium-high heat.

Step 3: Add marinated tofu to the skillet and cook until golden brown on all sides.

Step 4: Remove tofu from skillet and set aside.

Step 5: In the same skillet, add sliced vegetables such as bell peppers, broccoli, and carrots.

Step 6: Cook vegetables until tender-crisp.

Step 7: Add tofu back to the skillet and pour in more teriyaki sauce.

Step 8: Stir-fry everything together for a few minutes.

Step 9: Serve hot over cooked rice. Enjoy your teriyaki tofu stir-fry!

Helpful Tips:
1. Press the tofu for at least 30 minutes before cooking to remove excess water and ensure a firmer texture.

2. Cut the tofu into uniform cubes to ensure even cooking.

3. Use a non-stick skillet or wok to prevent sticking and achieve a crispy exterior.

4. Cook the tofu on high heat to achieve a nice sear and crispy texture.

5. Add your favorite vegetables such as bell peppers, broccoli, and snap peas for added flavor and nutrition.

6. Mix together soy sauce, ginger, garlic, and honey for a quick and easy teriyaki sauce.

7. Serve the stir-fry over steamed rice or noodles for a complete meal.

Baked halibut with herbs

Ingredients:
- 4 halibut fillets
- 2 tbsp olive oil
- 2 cloves garlic, minced
- 1 tbsp fresh parsley, chopped
- Salt and pepper to taste

Equipment:
1. Baking dish
2. Mixing bowl
3. Knife
4. Cutting board
5. Oven mitts

Methods:
Step 1: Preheat the oven to 375°F.

Step 2: Place the halibut fillets in a baking dish.

Step 3: Drizzle the fillets with olive oil and lemon juice.

Step 4: Season the fillets with salt, pepper, and your choice of herbs (such as parsley, dill, or thyme).

Step 5: Cover the baking dish with aluminum foil.

Step 6: Bake the halibut in the preheated oven for 15-20 minutes, or until the fish is opaque and flakes easily with a fork.

Step 7: Remove the foil and broil for an additional 2-3 minutes to brown the top.

Step 8: Serve the baked halibut hot with lemon wedges.

Helpful Tips:
1. Preheat your oven to 400 degrees F.

2. Place halibut fillets in a baking dish and drizzle with olive oil.

3. Season the fish with your favorite herbs such as dill, parsley, and lemon zest.

4. Squeeze fresh lemon juice over the fillets for added flavor.

5. Cover the baking dish with foil and bake for 15-20 minutes, or until the fish is cooked through and flakes easily with a fork.

6. For a crispy top, broil uncovered for an additional 2-3 minutes.

7. Serve hot with a side of roasted vegetables or a fresh salad. Enjoy!

Quinoa and black bean bowl

Ingredients:

- 1 cup quinoa
- 1 can black beans
- 1 avocado
- 1 lime

Equipment:

1. Knife
2. Cutting board
3. Saucepan
4. Wooden spoon
5. Spatula
6. Mixing bowl

Methods:

Step 1: Rinse 1 cup of quinoa under cold water until water runs clear.

Step 2: In a medium saucepan, bring 2 cups of water to a boil.

Step 3: Add quinoa to boiling water, cover, and reduce heat to low. Simmer for 15 minutes.

Step 4: In a separate pan, heat 1 tablespoon of olive oil over medium heat.

Step 5: Add 1 diced onion and 2 minced garlic cloves to the pan. Cook until onions are translucent.

Step 6: Add 1 can of drained and rinsed black beans to the onion mixture.

Step 7: Remove quinoa from heat and fluff with a fork.

Step 8: Serve quinoa topped with black bean mixture and your favorite toppings like avocado, salsa, and cilantro. Enjoy!

Helpful Tips:

1. Rinse the quinoa before cooking to remove any bitterness.
2. Use vegetable broth instead of water for added flavor.
3. Cook the quinoa according to package instructions, typically a 2:1 ratio of liquid to quinoa.

4. Season the black beans with cumin, chili powder, and garlic for a Mexican-inspired flavor.

5. Top the bowl with fresh avocado, cilantro, and lime juice for a burst of freshness.

6. Optional add-ins include corn, diced bell peppers, and shredded cheese.

7. Store any leftovers in an airtight container in the refrigerator for up to 3 days.

Chicken and vegetable lettuce wraps

Ingredients:

- 1 lb of chicken breast
- 1 red bell pepper, diced
- 1 zucchini, sliced
- 1 carrot, grated
- 1/4 cup soy sauce
- 1 tbsp sesame oil
- 1 head of lettuce

Equipment:

1. Knife
2. Cutting board
3. Frying pan
4. Mixing bowl
5. Tongs

Methods:

Step 1: Heat a small amount of oil in a pan over medium heat.

Step 2: Add bite-sized pieces of chicken to the pan and cook until browned and cooked through.

Step 3: Add diced vegetables such as bell peppers, carrots, and water chestnuts to the pan and cook until softened.

Step 4: Season with soy sauce, ginger, garlic, and a pinch of sugar for flavor.

Step 5: Spoon the chicken and vegetable mixture onto lettuce leaves.

Step 6: Garnish with chopped peanuts, cilantro, and a squeeze of lime juice.

Step 7: Roll up the lettuce leaves and enjoy your delicious chicken and vegetable lettuce wraps.

Helpful Tips:

1. Start by marinating the chicken in a tangy, Asian-inspired sauce for extra flavor.

2. Use a mix of crunchy vegetables like carrots, bell peppers, and water chestnuts for texture.

3. Cook the chicken until it is thoroughly cooked with no pink inside.

4. Serve the lettuce wraps with a side of rice or noodles for a complete meal.

5. Garnish with fresh herbs like cilantro or mint for a burst of freshness.

6. Don't forget to offer a variety of sauces like hoisin, sriracha, or soy sauce for dipping. Enjoy!

Lentil and spinach soup

Ingredients:

- 1 cup green lentils
- 4 cups vegetable broth
- 1 onion, chopped
- 2 cloves garlic, minced
- 4 cups fresh spinach leaves

Equipment:

1. Pot
2. Ladle
3. Wooden spoon
4. Blender
5. Knife

Methods:

Step 1: Rinse 1 cup of green lentils and set aside.

Step 2: In a large pot, heat 1 tablespoon of olive oil over medium heat.

Step 3: Add 1 diced onion and 2 minced garlic cloves and sauté until softened.

Step 4: Stir in 1 teaspoon of cumin, 1 teaspoon of coriander, and 1/2 teaspoon of smoked paprika.

Step 5: Pour in 4 cups of vegetable broth and the rinsed lentils.

Step 6: Bring to a boil, then reduce heat and simmer for 20 minutes.

Step 7: Add 3 cups of chopped spinach and cook until wilted.

Step 8: Season with salt and pepper to taste before serving.

Helpful Tips:

1. Start by sautéing onions, garlic, and carrots in oil until they are soft.

2. Add in lentils, vegetable broth, and diced tomatoes to the pot and bring to a boil.

3. Reduce heat and let simmer for about 20 minutes, until lentils are tender.

4. Stir in fresh spinach and cook until wilted.

5. Season with salt, pepper, and any desired herbs or spices.

6. For extra flavor, consider adding a squeeze of lemon juice or a splash of balsamic vinegar before serving.

7. Garnish with a dollop of Greek yogurt or a sprinkle of Parmesan cheese for a creamy finish.

8. Enjoy your nutritious and delicious Lentil and Spinach Soup!

Grilled tilapia with lemon caper sauce

Ingredients:
- 4 tilapia fillets
- 2 lemons
- 2 tbsp capers
- 4 tbsp olive oil
- Salt and pepper to taste

Equipment:
1. Grill
2. Tongs
3. Spatula
4. Lemon squeezer
5. Saucepan
6. Mixing bowl

Methods:
Step 1: Preheat grill to medium-high heat.

Step 2: Season tilapia fillets with salt and pepper.

Step 3: Grill tilapia fillets for 4-5 minutes per side, or until fish flakes easily with a fork.

Step 4: In a small saucepan, melt butter over medium heat.

Step 5: Add capers, lemon juice, and chicken broth to the saucepan.

Step 6: Simmer sauce for 3-4 minutes, or until slightly thickened.

Step 7: Remove sauce from heat and stir in chopped parsley.

Step 8: Serve grilled tilapia topped with lemon caper sauce. Enjoy!

Helpful Tips:
1. Preheat your grill to medium-high heat.

2. Season the tilapia fillets with salt, pepper, and a bit of olive oil before grilling.

3. Cook the fish for about 4-5 minutes per side, or until it flakes easily with a fork.

4. In a small saucepan, combine lemon juice, capers, minced garlic, and a splash of white wine.

5. Simmer the sauce for a few minutes until it thickens slightly.

6. Serve the grilled tilapia hot off the grill with the lemon caper sauce drizzled over the top.

7. Garnish with fresh parsley or lemon slices for added flavor and presentation. Enjoy!

Turkey and broccoli stir-fry

Ingredients:
- 1 lb turkey breast, thinly sliced
- 2 cups broccoli florets
- 1 red bell pepper, sliced
- 3 cloves garlic, minced
- 1/4 cup soy sauce
- 1 tbsp olive oil
- Salt and pepper to taste

Equipment:
1. Wok
2. Spatula
3. Cutting board
4. Knife
5. Tongs

Methods:
Step 1: Heat a large skillet over medium-high heat with olive oil.

Step 2: Add chopped turkey breast and cook until browned on all sides.

Step 3: Remove turkey from skillet and set aside.

Step 4: In the same skillet, add chopped broccoli florets and cook until slightly tender.

Step 5: Add back the turkey to the skillet.

Step 6: In a small bowl, mix together soy sauce, ginger, garlic, and honey.

Step 7: Pour the sauce over the turkey and broccoli.

Step 8: Stir-fry for another few minutes until everything is coated and heated through.

Step 9: Serve hot with rice or noodles.

Helpful Tips:
1. Start by marinating thin slices of turkey with soy sauce, garlic, and ginger for extra flavor.

2. Cook turkey in a hot skillet until browned and cooked through before adding vegetables.

3. Use high heat to stir-fry broccoli until tender-crisp, about 4-5 minutes.

4. Add a sauce made of soy sauce, oyster sauce, and a touch of honey for a savory and slightly sweet flavor.

5. Finish with a sprinkle of sesame seeds or chopped green onions for a pop of color and extra flavor.

6. Serve over steamed rice or noodles for a complete meal.

Tofu and vegetable curry

Ingredients:
- 1 block of tofu
- 1 onion
- 2 bell peppers
- 1 zucchini
- 1 can of coconut milk
- 2 tbsp curry powder
- 1 tbsp soy sauce
- 1 tbsp coconut oil

Equipment:
1. Knife
2. Cutting board
3. Saucepan
4. Wooden spoon
5. Serving spoon
6. Ladle

Methods:
Step 1: Heat oil in a large pot over medium heat.

Step 2: Add diced onion, minced garlic, and grated ginger to the pot, sauté until fragrant.

Step 3: Mix in curry powder, turmeric, and cumin, cook for another minute.

Step 4: Stir in diced tofu and chopped vegetables (such as bell peppers, broccoli, and carrots).

Step 5: Pour in coconut milk and vegetable broth, bring to a simmer.

Step 6: Cover and let it cook for 20-25 minutes, until vegetables are tender.

Step 7: Serve over rice or with naan bread, garnish with cilantro and lime wedges. Enjoy!

Helpful Tips:

BRINTALOS GEORGIOS

1. Press the tofu by wrapping it in paper towels and placing a heavy object on top to remove excess moisture before cooking.

2. Use a variety of colorful vegetables like bell peppers, carrots, broccoli, and zucchini for added flavor and nutrients.

3. Start by sautéing onions, garlic, and ginger in a pan before adding in the tofu and vegetables.

4. Add curry powder, turmeric, cumin, and coriander for a fragrant and flavorful spice blend.

5. Finish off the dish with a splash of coconut milk and a squeeze of fresh lime juice for a creamy and tangy finish.

Baked chicken parmesan

Ingredients:
- 4 boneless, skinless chicken breasts
- 1 cup breadcrumbs
- 1 cup grated Parmesan cheese
- 2 cups marinara sauce

Equipment:
1. Baking dish
2. Skillet
3. Tongs
4. Mixing bowl
5. Baking sheet

Methods:
Step 1: Preheat the oven to 400°F.

Step 2: Mix together breadcrumbs, grated parmesan cheese, salt, and pepper in a bowl.

Step 3: Dip each chicken breast in beaten eggs, then coat with the breadcrumb mixture.

Step 4: Place the coated chicken breasts on a baking sheet.

Step 5: Bake in the preheated oven for 20-25 minutes, or until the chicken is cooked through.

Step 6: Top each chicken breast with marinara sauce and mozzarella cheese.

Step 7: Return the chicken to the oven and bake for an additional 5-10 minutes, or until the cheese is melted and bubbly.

Step 8: Serve hot and enjoy!

Helpful Tips:
1. Pound chicken breasts to an even thickness for even cooking.

2. Dip chicken in flour, then beaten eggs, and finally breadcrumbs for a crispy exterior.

3. Use a baking sheet lined with parchment paper to prevent sticking.

4. Bake at a high temperature (around 400°F) to ensure a crispy crust.

5. Top with marinara sauce and mozzarella cheese towards the end of cooking to prevent burning.

6. Let the dish rest for a few minutes before serving to allow the flavors to meld.

7. Serve with pasta or a fresh salad for a balanced meal.

Lentil and vegetable salad

Ingredients:

- 1 cup cooked lentils
- 1 red bell pepper, diced
- 1 cucumber, diced
- 1/4 red onion, chopped
- 1/4 cup feta cheese
- 2 tbsp olive oil
- 1 tbsp balsamic vinegar
- Salt and pepper to taste

Equipment:

1. Knife
2. Cutting board
3. Mixing bowl
4. Salad spinner
5. Serving spoon

Methods:

Step 1: Rinse 1 cup of lentils and cook according to package instructions.

Step 2: Chop up your favorite vegetables (such as red pepper, cucumber, and cherry tomatoes).

Step 3: In a large bowl, mix together the cooked lentils and chopped vegetables.

Step 4: In a small bowl, whisk together olive oil, lemon juice, salt, and pepper to make a dressing.

Step 5: Pour the dressing over the lentil and vegetable mixture and toss well to combine.

Step 6: Let the salad sit for about 15 minutes to allow the flavors to meld.

Step 7: Serve and enjoy your delicious Lentil and vegetable salad!

Helpful Tips:

1. Start by cooking lentils according to package instructions and allow to cool.

2. Chop a variety of colorful vegetables such as bell peppers, cucumbers, cherry tomatoes, and red onions.

3. Mix the cooked lentils and chopped vegetables in a large bowl.

4. Drizzle with olive oil, lemon juice, and your favorite herbs and spices for added flavor.

5. Feel free to add other ingredients like feta cheese, olives, or avocado for a creamy texture.

6. Serve chilled and enjoy as a healthy and filling meal for lunch or dinner.

Shrimp and vegetable stir-fry

Ingredients:

- 1 lb shrimp
- 2 cups mixed vegetables
- 3 tbsp soy sauce
- 2 cloves garlic
- 1 tsp ginger
- 1 tbsp oil

Equipment:

1. Wok
2. Spatula
3. Knife
4. Cutting board
5. Tongs

Methods:

Step 1: Heat oil in a large skillet or wok over medium-high heat.

Step 2: Add thinly sliced bell peppers, broccoli florets, and snow peas to the skillet.

Step 3: Cook the vegetables for 3-4 minutes until they start to soften.

Step 4: Push the vegetables to one side of the skillet and add the shrimp.

Step 5: Cook the shrimp for 2-3 minutes until they turn pink and opaque.

Step 6: Combine the shrimp with the vegetables in the skillet.

Step 7: Add soy sauce, garlic, ginger, and a pinch of red pepper flakes.

Step 8: Stir-fry for an additional 2-3 minutes.

Step 9: Serve hot over rice or noodles. Enjoy!

Helpful Tips:

1. Start by preparing all your ingredients ahead of time to ensure a smooth cooking process.

2. Use a high heat when stir-frying to achieve a nice sear on the shrimp and vegetables.

3. Don't overcrowd the pan, cook in batches if needed to prevent steaming rather than frying the ingredients.

4. Add aromatics like garlic, ginger, and green onions for extra flavor.

5. Season with soy sauce, oyster sauce, and a touch of sugar for a perfect balance of sweet and savory flavors.

6. Serve over a bed of steamed rice or noodles for a complete meal.

Black bean and sweet potato chili

Ingredients:

- 1 onion, diced
- 2 cloves garlic, minced
- 1 sweet potato, cubed
- 1 can black beans
- 1 can diced tomatoes
- 1 tbsp chili powder
- 1 tsp cumin
- Salt and pepper to taste

Equipment:

1. Pot
2. Skillet
3. Spoon
4. Knife
5. Cutting board
6. Ladle

Methods:

Step 1: Heat olive oil in a large pot over medium heat.

Step 2: Add diced onions and cook until translucent.

Step 3: Stir in minced garlic and cook for another minute.

Step 4: Add diced sweet potatoes, black beans, diced tomatoes, vegetable broth, chili powder, cumin, and salt.

Step 5: Bring the mixture to a boil, then reduce heat and let simmer for about 30 minutes.

Step 6: Stir occasionally and adjust seasoning to taste.

Step 7: Serve hot, topped with your favorite garnishes such as avocado, cilantro, and lime wedges.

Step 8: Enjoy your delicious and hearty black bean and sweet potato chili!

Helpful Tips:

BRINTALOS GEORGIOS

1. Start by sautéing onions, garlic, and bell peppers in a large pot until softened.

2. Add in diced sweet potatoes, black beans, diced tomatoes, and vegetable broth.

3. Season with chili powder, cumin, smoked paprika, and salt to taste.

4. Simmer on low heat for at least 30 minutes to allow flavors to meld together.

5. For added heat, stir in diced jalapeños or a pinch of cayenne pepper.

6. Serve with toppings like avocado, cilantro, lime wedges, and crushed tortilla chips.

7. Consider making a double batch and freezing some for later for a quick and healthy meal.

Chicken piccata with lemon

Ingredients:

- 4 boneless, skinless chicken breasts
- 1/2 cup flour
- 2 lemons
- 1/4 cup capers
- 1/2 cup chicken broth
- 1/4 cup white wine
- Olive oil
- Salt and pepper

Equipment:

1. Skillet
2. Tongs
3. Knife
4. Cutting board
5. Lemon squeezer
6. Whisk

Methods:

Step 1: Pound chicken breasts to 1/4-inch thickness and season with salt and pepper.

Step 2: Dredge chicken in flour, shaking off excess.

Step 3: Heat olive oil in a large skillet over medium-high heat.

Step 4: Cook chicken until golden brown and cooked through, about 3-4 minutes per side.

Step 5: Remove chicken and set aside.

Step 6: In the same skillet, add chicken broth, lemon juice, and capers.

Step 7: Cook for 2 minutes, scraping up any browned bits from the pan.

Step 8: Return chicken to the skillet and simmer for 2 minutes.

Step 9: Serve chicken piccata with lemon slices on top. Enjoy!

Helpful Tips:

BRINTALOS GEORGIOS

1. Pound chicken breasts to even thickness for quicker and more even cooking.

2. Season the chicken with salt and pepper before dredging in flour to enhance flavor.

3. Cook chicken in a hot skillet with oil for a crispy exterior.

4. Make a flavorful sauce with chicken broth, white wine, lemon juice, capers, and butter.

5. Cook the sauce until thickened and reduced before pouring over the chicken.

6. Garnish with fresh parsley and lemon slices for a pop of color and added freshness.

7. Serve the chicken piccata over pasta or with a side of roasted vegetables for a complete meal.

Roasted eggplant salad

Ingredients:

- 2 eggplants
- 2 tbsp olive oil
- 1 tsp ground cumin
- Salt and pepper to taste
- 1/4 cup feta cheese
- Fresh parsley for garnish

Equipment:

1. Knife
2. Cutting board
3. Mixing bowl
4. Baking sheet
5. Tongs

Methods:

Step 1: Preheat your oven to 400°F.

Step 2: Cut an eggplant into cubes and place on a baking sheet.

Step 3: Drizzle olive oil over the eggplant and season with salt and pepper.

Step 4: Roast the eggplant in the oven for 25-30 minutes, or until tender and golden brown.

Step 5: In a separate bowl, mix together diced tomatoes, chopped cucumbers, red onion, and fresh herbs like parsley and mint.

Step 6: Once the eggplant is roasted, let it cool slightly before adding it to the bowl of vegetables.

Step 7: Toss everything together with a dressing made of olive oil, lemon juice, and garlic.

Step 8: Serve the roasted eggplant salad warm or at room temperature. Enjoy!

Helpful Tips:

1. Preheat your oven to 400°F before you start preparing the eggplant.
2. Cut the eggplant into uniform pieces to ensure even cooking.

3. Salt the eggplant slices and let them sit for 10-15 minutes to draw out excess moisture and bitterness.

4. Pat the eggplant dry with paper towels before roasting to prevent it from becoming soggy.

5. Drizzle olive oil over the eggplant slices and season with herbs and spices before roasting for added flavor.

6. Roast the eggplant until it is golden brown and tender, typically around 25-30 minutes.

7. Allow the roasted eggplant to cool slightly before tossing with your desired salad ingredients.

Broccoli and cheddar stuffed chicken

Ingredients:
- 4 boneless, skinless chicken breasts
- 1 cup broccoli florets
- 1 cup cheddar cheese
- Salt and pepper

(96 characters)

Equipment:
1. Knife
2. Cutting board
3. Mixing bowl
4. Baking dish
5. Tongs

Methods:
Step 1: Preheat your oven to 375°F.

Step 2: Season boneless, skinless chicken breasts with salt and pepper.

Step 3: Cut a slit into each chicken breast to create a pocket for the filling.

Step 4: Mix together chopped broccoli florets with shredded cheddar cheese.

Step 5: Stuff each chicken breast with the broccoli and cheddar mixture.

Step 6: Secure the opening with toothpicks.

Step 7: Place the stuffed chicken breasts in a baking dish.

Step 8: Bake for 25-30 minutes or until the chicken is cooked through.

Step 9: Remove the toothpicks before serving.

Step 10: Enjoy your delicious broccoli and cheddar stuffed chicken!

Helpful Tips:
1. Begin by pounding chicken breasts to an even thickness for even cooking.

2. Mix together chopped broccoli, shredded cheddar cheese, and seasonings as filling.

3. Carefully cut a pocket in the chicken breasts and stuff with broccoli and cheddar mixture.

4. Use toothpicks to secure the chicken pockets closed.

5. Bake chicken in the oven until cooked through, about 25-30 minutes at 375°F.

6. Serve with a side of roasted vegetables or a fresh salad for a complete meal.

Tofu and broccoli stir-fry

Ingredients:
- 1 block of tofu
- 2 cups of broccoli
- 2 tbsp soy sauce
- 1 tbsp sesame oil

Equipment:
1. Wok
2. Spatula
3. Knife
4. Cutting board
5. Stirring spoon

Methods:
Step 1: Press tofu to remove excess water, then cut into bite-sized cubes.

Step 2: Heat oil in a pan over medium heat.

Step 3: Add tofu cubes and cook until golden brown on all sides.

Step 4: Remove tofu from pan and set aside.

Step 5: In the same pan, add broccoli florets and stir-fry until slightly tender.

Step 6: Return tofu to the pan with broccoli.

Step 7: In a small bowl, mix together soy sauce, garlic, ginger, and sesame oil.

Step 8: Pour sauce over tofu and broccoli, stirring to combine.

Step 9: Cook for an additional 2-3 minutes, then serve hot.

Helpful Tips:
1. Drain the tofu and press it between paper towels to remove excess moisture before cooking.

2. Cut the tofu into small cubes to ensure even cooking.

3. Heat a non-stick pan or wok with a small amount of oil before adding the tofu cubes.

4. Stir-fry the tofu until it is golden brown and slightly crispy on the outside.

5. Add broccoli florets to the pan and stir-fry until they are tender-crisp.

6. Season the stir-fry with soy sauce, garlic, ginger, and a pinch of red pepper flakes for added flavor.

7. Serve the tofu and broccoli stir-fry over cooked rice or noodles for a complete meal.

Spicy shrimp lettuce wraps

Ingredients:
- 1 pound shrimp
- 1 head lettuce
- 1/4 cup soy sauce
- 2 cloves garlic
- 1 tablespoon Sriracha
- 1 tablespoon sesame oil

Equipment:
1. Knife
2. Cutting board
3. Skillet
4. Tongs
5. Mixing bowl

Methods:
Step 1: Marinate shrimp in a mixture of soy sauce, sriracha, garlic, and ginger.

Step 2: Heat oil in a pan and sauté the marinated shrimp until they are cooked through.

Step 3: Remove the shrimp from the pan and set aside.

Step 4: In the same pan, add chopped bell peppers, onions, and water chestnuts.

Step 5: Cook until the vegetables are tender.

Step 6: Add the cooked shrimp back into the pan and mix everything together.

Step 7: Serve the spicy shrimp mixture in lettuce leaves, garnished with chopped cilantro and peanuts.

Step 8: Enjoy your delicious and healthy spicy shrimp lettuce wraps!

Helpful Tips:
1. Marinate the shrimp in a spicy mixture of chili flakes, garlic, ginger, and soy sauce for at least 30 minutes.

2. Use a high heat when cooking the shrimp to get a nice sear and prevent overcooking.

3. Double up on the lettuce leaves to prevent the filling from leaking out.

4. Serve with a side of sliced cucumbers or avocado for a refreshing contrast to the spice.

5. Garnish with fresh cilantro, lime wedges, and crushed peanuts for added flavor and texture.

6. Customize the level of heat by adjusting the amount of chili flakes or hot sauce used.

Lentil and beet salad

Ingredients:
- 1 cup cooked lentils
- 2 beets, peeled and chopped
- 1/4 cup feta cheese
- 2 tbsp balsamic vinegar
- Salt and pepper to taste

Equipment:
1. Mixing bowl
2. Whisk
3. Cutting board
4. Knife
5. Salad spinner

Methods:

Step 1: Rinse 1 cup of lentils and cook in a pot with 2 cups of water for about 20 minutes.

Step 2: Peel and dice 3 medium beets, then roast in the oven at 400°F for 25-30 minutes.

Step 3: In a small bowl, whisk together 3 tbsp of olive oil, 2 tbsp of balsamic vinegar, 1 tsp of Dijon mustard, and a pinch of salt and pepper.

Step 4: Combine the cooked lentils, roasted beets, and dressing in a large bowl.

Step 5: Toss well to coat everything evenly.

Step 6: Serve the salad chilled or at room temperature. Enjoy!

Helpful Tips:

1. Start by cooking the lentils according to package instructions until tender but slightly firm.

2. Roast or boil the beets until they are easily pierced with a fork, then peel and dice them.

3. Mix the lentils and beets in a large bowl with some chopped parsley, crumbled feta cheese, and a dressing of balsamic vinegar, olive oil, salt, and pepper.

4. Let the salad sit for at least 30 minutes before serving to allow the flavors to meld together.

5. Feel free to add other ingredients like chopped nuts, avocado, or fresh herbs for additional texture and flavor.

Grilled turkey burgers

Ingredients:

- 1 pound ground turkey
- 1/4 cup bread crumbs
- 1/4 cup grated Parmesan cheese
- 1/4 cup chopped parsley
- 1 teaspoon garlic powder
- Salt and pepper to taste
- 4 hamburger buns

Equipment:

1. Grill
2. Spatula
3. Tongs
4. Cutting Board
5. Knife

Methods:

Step 1: Preheat your grill to medium-high heat.

Step 2: In a large mixing bowl, combine ground turkey, breadcrumbs, chopped onions, garlic powder, salt, and pepper.

Step 3: Form the mixture into burger patties of desired size.

Step 4: Place the turkey burgers on the grill and cook for 4-5 minutes per side.

Step 5: Check the internal temperature of the burgers to ensure they are cooked to at least 165°F.

Step 6: Remove the burgers from the grill and let them rest for a few minutes before serving.

Step 7: Serve the grilled turkey burgers on buns with your favorite toppings and enjoy!

Helpful Tips:

1. Start by selecting lean ground turkey to make healthier burgers.

2. Mix in your favorite seasonings, such as garlic powder, onion powder, and black pepper, for added flavor.

3. Form your patties evenly to ensure they cook evenly on the grill.

4. Preheat your grill to medium-high heat before placing the burgers on.

5. Cook the turkey burgers for about 5-7 minutes per side, or until they reach an internal temperature of 165°F.

6. Add your favorite toppings, such as lettuce, tomato, and avocado, before serving.

7. Enjoy your delicious grilled turkey burgers with a side of sweet potato fries or a fresh salad!

Vegetable and quinoa soup

Ingredients:

- 1 cup quinoa
- 1 onion
- 2 carrots
- 2 stalks celery
- 1 zucchini
- 1 can diced tomatoes
- 6 cups vegetable broth
- Salt, pepper, and herbs

Equipment:

1. Pot
2. Ladle
3. Chef's knife
4. Cutting board
5. Wooden spoon

Methods:

Step 1: In a medium pot, heat olive oil over medium heat.

Step 2: Add chopped onions and garlic, sauté until onions are translucent.

Step 3: Add chopped carrots, celery, and bell pepper, cook for a few minutes.

Step 4: Pour in vegetable broth and bring to a boil.

Step 5: Stir in quinoa and reduce heat to simmer for 15-20 minutes.

Step 6: Add chopped kale and let it cook for 5 more minutes.

Step 7: Season with salt, pepper, and any other desired herbs or spices.

Step 8: Serve hot and enjoy your delicious vegetable and quinoa soup.

Helpful Tips:

1. Start by sautéing onions and garlic in olive oil for added flavor.

2. Use a variety of colorful vegetables like carrots, bell peppers, and spinach for a nutritious soup.

3. Rinse quinoa before adding it to the soup to remove any bitterness.

4. Season with herbs and spices like thyme, oregano, and cumin for a flavorful taste.

5. Don't overcook the vegetables to maintain their texture and nutrients.

6. Add a splash of vegetable broth or water if the soup becomes too thick.

7. Garnish with fresh herbs or a sprinkle of Parmesan cheese before serving.

Baked lemon pepper cod

Ingredients:
- 4 cod fillets
- 2 tbsp lemon juice
- 1 tbsp olive oil
- 1 tsp black pepper
- Salt to taste

Equipment:
1. Baking dish
2. Mixing bowl
3. Whisk
4. Basting brush
5. Oven mitts

Methods:
Step 1: Preheat the oven to 400°F.

Step 2: Season the cod fillets with lemon pepper seasoning, salt, and pepper.

Step 3: Place the cod fillets in a baking dish.

Step 4: Drizzle olive oil over the fillets.

Step 5: Squeeze fresh lemon juice over the fillets.

Step 6: Bake the cod in the preheated oven for 15-20 minutes, or until the fish is cooked through and flakes easily with a fork.

Step 7: Optional - garnish with fresh parsley or additional lemon slices before serving.

Step 8: Enjoy your delicious baked lemon pepper cod!

Helpful Tips:
1. Preheat your oven to 400°F and lightly grease a baking dish.

2. Season cod fillets with lemon pepper seasoning, salt, and a drizzle of olive oil.

3. Place the seasoned cod in the prepared baking dish.

4. Squeeze fresh lemon juice over the cod for extra flavor.

5. Bake in the preheated oven for 12-15 minutes, or until the fish flakes easily with a fork.

6. Serve the baked lemon pepper cod with a side of steamed vegetables or a fresh salad.

7. Garnish with fresh herbs like parsley or dill for a pop of color and added freshness.

Chicken and vegetable kebabs

Ingredients:

- 1 lb boneless, skinless chicken breasts
- 1 red bell pepper
- 1 yellow bell pepper
- 1 zucchini
- 1 red onion
- 1/4 cup olive oil
- 2 tbsp balsamic vinegar
- Salt and pepper to taste

Equipment:

1. Skewers
2. Tongs
3. Grilling pan
4. Basting brush
5. Cutting board
6. Knife

Methods:

Step 1: Cut boneless chicken thighs into bite-sized pieces

Step 2: Marinate chicken pieces with olive oil, lemon juice, garlic, and herbs

Step 3: Cut vegetables like bell peppers, onions, and zucchini into chunks

Step 4: Thread chicken and vegetable pieces onto skewers

Step 5: Preheat grill to medium-high heat

Step 6: Grill kebabs for 10-15 minutes, turning occasionally until chicken is cooked through

Step 7: Serve hot with a side of rice or salad

Step 8: Enjoy your delicious and healthy chicken and vegetable kebabs!

Helpful Tips:

1. Marinate the chicken in a mixture of lemon juice, olive oil, garlic, and herbs for at least an hour before grilling.

2. Skewer the chicken and vegetables separately to ensure even cooking.

3. Pre-cook denser vegetables like potatoes or carrots before skewering to ensure they cook through.

4. Soak wooden skewers in water for at least 30 minutes to prevent them from burning on the grill.

5. Rotate the kebabs every few minutes to ensure they cook evenly on all sides.

6. Serve the kebabs with tzatziki sauce or a yogurt-based dressing for added flavor.

7. Enjoy your delicious and healthy meal!

Green bean and chicken stir-fry

Ingredients:

- 1 lb of chicken breast
- 1 lb of green beans
- 1 bell pepper
- 1/4 cup of soy sauce
- 2 cloves of garlic
- 1 tsp of ginger

Equipment:

1. Wok
2. Wooden spoon
3. Cutting board
4. Knife
5. Tongs

Methods:

Step 1: Cut 1 pound of chicken breast into bite-sized pieces.

Step 2: Heat 2 tablespoons of oil in a large skillet over medium heat.

Step 3: Add the chicken pieces and cook until browned and cooked through. Remove from skillet.

Step 4: In the same skillet, add 1 pound of green beans (trimmed and cut into 2-inch pieces).

Step 5: Stir-fry the green beans for 5-7 minutes or until they are crisp-tender.

Step 6: Add the cooked chicken back to the skillet.

Step 7: In a small bowl, mix together ¼ cup soy sauce, 2 tablespoons of hoisin sauce, and 1 tablespoon of sesame oil.

Step 8: Pour the sauce over the chicken and green beans, stirring to coat.

Step 9: Cook for an additional 2-3 minutes, until heated through.

Step 10: Serve the green bean and chicken stir-fry hot over rice or noodles. Enjoy!

Helpful Tips:

BRINTALOS GEORGIOS

1. Start by preparing all your ingredients beforehand: green beans, chicken, garlic, ginger, soy sauce, sesame oil, and any other desired vegetables.

2. Cut chicken into bite-sized pieces and season with salt and pepper before stir-frying in a hot pan.

3. Add garlic and ginger to the pan once the chicken is cooked through to infuse flavor.

4. Toss in green beans and other vegetables, and stir-fry until they are crisp-tender.

5. Drizzle with soy sauce and sesame oil for added flavor.

6. Serve over rice or noodles for a complete meal. Enjoy your delicious green bean and chicken stir-fry!

Grilled shrimp salad

Ingredients:
- 1 lb large shrimp
- 4 cups mixed greens
- 1 avocado, sliced
- 1 cup cherry tomatoes
- 1/4 cup balsamic vinaigrette dressing

Equipment:
1. Grilling pan
2. Tongs
3. Salad spinner
4. Cutting board
5. Mixing bowl

Methods:
Step 1: Preheat the grill to medium-high heat.

Step 2: Clean and peel the shrimp, removing the shells and tails.

Step 3: In a bowl, toss the shrimp with olive oil, garlic, salt, pepper, and any other desired seasonings.

Step 4: Thread the shrimp onto skewers for easier grilling.

Step 5: Grill the shrimp for 2-3 minutes per side, until pink and cooked through.

Step 6: Remove the shrimp from the grill and let cool.

Step 7: In a large bowl, toss together mixed greens, cherry tomatoes, sliced cucumbers, and any other desired salad ingredients.

Step 8: Top the salad with the grilled shrimp and serve with your favorite dressing.

Helpful Tips:
1. Marinate shrimp in olive oil, garlic, lemon and herbs for at least 30 minutes before grilling.

2. Preheat the grill to medium-high heat to ensure perfectly cooked shrimp.

3. Skewer the shrimp before grilling to make them easier to flip.

4. Grill shrimp for 2-3 minutes per side until they turn pink and opaque.

5. Toss the grilled shrimp with mixed greens, cherry tomatoes, avocado and a light vinaigrette for a refreshing salad.

6. Optional toppings can include feta cheese, toasted nuts or seeds for added flavor and texture.

7. Serve the salad immediately to enjoy the shrimp at their best.

Tofu and vegetable noodle bowl

Ingredients:
- 1 firm tofu block (14 oz)
- 8 oz rice noodles
- 2 cups mixed vegetables
- 1/4 cup soy sauce
- 2 tbsp sesame oil
- 1 tsp ginger
- 1 garlic clove

Equipment:
1. Cutting board
2. Knife
3. Pot
4. Colander
5. Wok
6. Tongs

Methods:
Step 1: Boil water in a pot and add in your desired noodles. Cook according to package instructions.

Step 2: While the noodles are cooking, heat a skillet with oil over medium heat.

Step 3: Add in diced tofu and cook until golden brown on all sides.

Step 4: Remove tofu from the skillet and set aside.

Step 5: In the same skillet, add in your favorite vegetables such as bell peppers, broccoli, and carrots. Cook until tender.

Step 6: In a small bowl, mix together soy sauce, garlic, and ginger.

Step 7: Add the tofu back to the skillet and pour the sauce over the tofu and vegetables.

Step 8: Serve the tofu and vegetable mixture over the cooked noodles. Enjoy your delicious tofu and vegetable noodle bowl!

Helpful Tips:

BRINTALOS GEORGIOS

1. Press tofu before cooking to remove excess water and improve texture.

2. Use firm or extra firm tofu for better consistency in the noodle bowl.

3. Marinate tofu in soy sauce, garlic, and other seasonings for added flavor.

4. Stir-fry tofu in a hot pan with some oil until crispy on the outside.

5. Add a variety of colorful vegetables like bell peppers, broccoli, and carrots for a nutrient-packed meal.

6. Cook noodles separately and toss with the tofu and vegetables at the end.

7. Garnish with fresh herbs, peanuts, or sesame seeds for extra taste and texture.

Baked turkey tenderloin

Ingredients:

- 1 lb turkey tenderloin
- 2 cloves garlic, minced
- 1 tbsp olive oil
- 1 tsp salt
- 1/2 tsp black pepper
- 1/2 tsp paprika
- 1/2 tsp dried thyme

Equipment:

1. Baking sheet
2. Roasting pan
3. Meat thermometer
4. Basting brush
5. Oven mitts

Methods:

Step 1: Preheat the oven to 375°F.

Step 2: Season the turkey tenderloin with salt, pepper, and any other desired seasonings.

Step 3: Place the seasoned turkey tenderloin in a baking dish or on a lined baking sheet.

Step 4: Add some broth or water to the bottom of the dish to keep the turkey tenderloin moist.

Step 5: Cover the baking dish with aluminum foil.

Step 6: Bake the turkey tenderloin in the preheated oven for about 30-40 minutes, or until it reaches an internal temperature of 165°F.

Step 7: Remove the turkey tenderloin from the oven and let it rest for 5-10 minutes before slicing and serving. Enjoy!

Helpful Tips:

1. Preheat your oven to 375°F.

2. Season the turkey tenderloin with salt, pepper, and any desired herbs or spices.

3. Place the tenderloin in a roasting pan and drizzle with olive oil or melted butter.

4. Bake uncovered for 25-30 minutes or until the internal temperature reaches 165°F.

5. Let the turkey rest for 5-10 minutes before slicing and serving.

6. For added flavor, consider basting the tenderloin with a mixture of chicken broth and herbs during baking.

7. Serve with your favorite sides, such as roasted vegetables or garlic mashed potatoes.

Bean and barley soup

Ingredients:
- 1 cup dried beans
- 1/2 cup barley
- 1 onion
- 2 carrots
- 2 celery stalks
- 4 cups vegetable broth
- 2 garlic cloves
- Salt and pepper to taste

Equipment:
1. Ladle
2. Stockpot
3. Immersion blender
4. Cutting board
5. Chef's knife

Methods:
Step 1: Rinse 1 cup of barley under cold water and set aside.

Step 2: In a large pot, heat 1 tablespoon of olive oil over medium heat.

Step 3: Add 1 diced onion, 2 minced garlic cloves, and 2 diced carrots to the pot.

Step 4: Cook until vegetables are soft, about 5 minutes.

Step 5: Add 6 cups of vegetable broth, rinsed barley, 1 can of diced tomatoes, and 1 can of drained and rinsed beans to the pot.

Step 6: Bring to a boil, then reduce heat and simmer for 45 minutes.

Step 7: Season with salt and pepper to taste.

Step 8: Serve hot and enjoy!

Helpful Tips:
1. Rinse the beans and barley thoroughly before cooking to remove any debris.

2. Soak the beans overnight to help shorten cooking time and improve digestibility.

3. Use a mix of beans such as kidney beans, black beans, and navy beans for variety in texture and flavor.

4. Add aromatics like onions, garlic, and carrots for depth of flavor.

5. Season with herbs like thyme, rosemary, and bay leaves for added complexity.

6. Consider adding diced tomatoes or tomato paste for a tangy element.

7. Cook on low heat for at least an hour to allow the flavors to meld together.

Teriyaki salmon with vegetables

Ingredients:

- 4 salmon fillets
- 1/2 cup soy sauce
- 1/4 cup brown sugar
- 2 cloves garlic, minced
- 1 tsp ginger, grated
- 4 cups mixed vegetables

Equipment:

1. Frying pan
2. Spatula
3. Chef's knife
4. Cutting board
5. Baking sheet

Methods:

Step 1: Preheat the oven to 400°F.

Step 2: Season salmon fillets with salt and pepper.

Step 3: In a small bowl, whisk together teriyaki sauce, soy sauce, honey, ginger, and garlic.

Step 4: Place salmon fillets in a baking dish and pour the teriyaki sauce mixture over them.

Step 5: Add sliced vegetables like bell peppers, zucchini, and carrots to the baking dish.

Step 6: Cover the baking dish with foil and bake in the preheated oven for 20-25 minutes.

Step 7: Remove the foil and broil for an additional 5 minutes to caramelize the top of the salmon.

Step 8: Serve the teriyaki salmon and vegetables over steamed rice. Enjoy!

Helpful Tips:

1. Marinate salmon fillets in teriyaki sauce for at least 30 minutes before cooking.

2. Preheat oven to 400°F and line a baking sheet with foil for easy cleanup.

3. Chop a variety of your favorite vegetables such as bell peppers, broccoli, and carrots.

4. Toss vegetables in a bit of olive oil, salt, and pepper before arranging them on the baking sheet.

5. Place marinated salmon fillets on top of the vegetables.

6. Bake for 15-20 minutes or until salmon is cooked through and vegetables are tender.

7. Serve hot with rice or quinoa for a complete meal. Enjoy!

Quinoa and spinach salad

Ingredients:

- 1 cup quinoa
- 2 cups baby spinach
- 1/2 cup cherry tomatoes
- 1/4 cup feta cheese
- 1/4 cup balsamic vinaigrette dressing

Equipment:

1. Knife
2. Cutting board
3. Mixing bowl
4. Salad spinner
5. Fork
6. Serving platter

Methods:

Step 1: Rinse 1 cup of quinoa under cold water

Step 2: In a medium saucepan, bring 2 cups of water to a boil

Step 3: Add quinoa to boiling water, cover, and simmer for 15 minutes

Step 4: Remove from heat and let quinoa sit for 5 minutes, then fluff with a fork

Step 5: In a large bowl, combine cooked quinoa with 2 cups of chopped spinach

Step 6: Add 1 diced red bell pepper, 1/4 cup of chopped red onion, and 1/4 cup of crumbled feta cheese

Step 7: In a small bowl, whisk together 1/4 cup of olive oil, 2 tablespoons of red wine vinegar, and salt and pepper to taste

Step 8: Pour dressing over salad and toss to combine

Step 9: Serve chilled and enjoy your quinoa and spinach salad!

Helpful Tips:

1. Rinse the quinoa before cooking to remove any bitterness.
2. Cook the quinoa in vegetable or chicken broth for added flavor.

3. Let the cooked quinoa cool before mixing with the other salad ingredients to prevent wilting the spinach.

4. Dress the salad with a simple vinaigrette or lemon juice and olive oil for a light and refreshing flavor.

5. Add in additional veggies like cherry tomatoes, cucumbers, and bell peppers for extra crunch and nutrition.

6. Top with feta cheese, nuts, or seeds for added texture and protein.

Roasted vegetable and chicken pasta

Ingredients:
- 1 lb chicken breast
- 2 cups mixed vegetables
- 8 oz pasta
- 1/4 cup olive oil
- Salt and pepper to taste

Equipment:
1. Pot
2. Pan
3. Wooden spoon
4. Colander
5. Tongs

Methods:
Step 1: Preheat the oven to 400°F.

Step 2: Chop your choice of vegetables (such as bell peppers, zucchini, and cherry tomatoes) and place them on a baking sheet.

Step 3: Season the vegetables with salt, pepper, and olive oil.

Step 4: Place chicken breast seasoned with salt and pepper on the same baking sheet.

Step 5: Roast the vegetables and chicken in the oven for 20-25 minutes, or until cooked through.

Step 6: Meanwhile, cook your favorite pasta according to package instructions.

Step 7: Once the chicken and vegetables are done, chop the chicken into bite-sized pieces.

Step 8: Toss the roasted vegetables, chicken, and cooked pasta together in a large bowl.

Step 9: Serve hot and enjoy your delicious roasted vegetable and chicken pasta!

Helpful Tips:

BRINTALOS GEORGIOS

1. Preheat your oven to 400°F before you start preparing your vegetables and chicken.

2. Cut your vegetables into uniform sizes to ensure even roasting.

3. Toss your vegetables and chicken with olive oil, salt, pepper, and any desired herbs/spices before placing them on a baking sheet.

4. Place the baking sheet in the center rack of the oven to ensure even cooking.

5. Check your vegetables and chicken periodically to prevent burning, and rotate the baking sheet if needed.

6. Cook your pasta according to package instructions and save some pasta water to loosen the sauce if needed.

7. Mix your roasted vegetables and chicken with the cooked pasta, adding in some Parmesan cheese and fresh herbs for extra flavor. Enjoy!

Low-fat turkey and bean stew

Ingredients:
- 1 lb ground turkey
- 1 can kidney beans
- 1 can diced tomatoes
- 1 onion
- 2 cloves garlic
- 1 tsp cumin
- 1 tsp paprika
- 4 cups chicken broth

Equipment:
1. Knife
2. Cutting board
3. Pot
4. Wooden spoon
5. Ladle

Methods:
Step 1: Heat olive oil in a large pot over medium heat.

Step 2: Add diced onions, garlic, and celery and sauté until softened.

Step 3: Stir in ground turkey and cook until browned.

Step 4: Add diced tomatoes, kidney beans, and chicken broth to the pot.

Step 5: Season with salt, pepper, cumin, and paprika.

Step 6: Bring the stew to a simmer and let it cook for 20-30 minutes.

Step 7: Stir in chopped spinach and cook for an additional 5 minutes.

Step 8: Adjust seasoning if needed.

Step 9: Serve the turkey and bean stew hot and enjoy the low-fat and nutritious meal!

Helpful Tips:
1. Start by using lean ground turkey instead of higher-fat options like ground beef.

2. Use low-sodium chicken broth to help control the amount of salt in the dish.

3. Add plenty of vegetables like carrots, onions, and celery to bulk up the stew without adding extra fat.

4. Consider using dried herbs and spices for flavor instead of additional fats like butter or oils.

5. Drain and rinse canned beans to reduce their sodium content before adding them to the stew.

6. Serve the stew with whole grain bread or a side salad for a balanced meal.

Grilled tofu tacos

Ingredients:
- 1 block tofu
- 1/4 cup soy sauce
- 2 tbsp olive oil
- 1 tbsp chili powder
- 1 tsp cumin
- 1/2 tsp garlic powder
- 1/2 tsp paprika
- 1/4 tsp salt
- 1/4 tsp pepper

Equipment:
1. Grill pan
2. Tongs
3. Chef's knife
4. Cutting board
5. Mixing bowl

Methods:
Step 1: Press tofu to remove excess water for at least 30 minutes.

Step 2: Slice tofu into even strips and marinate in a mixture of soy sauce, lime juice, and spices for 1 hour.

Step 3: Preheat grill to medium-high heat and lightly oil grates.

Step 4: Grill tofu for 3-4 minutes per side, until browned and slightly charred.

Step 5: Warm corn tortillas on the grill for 30 seconds on each side.

Step 6: Assemble tacos with grilled tofu, avocado, salsa, cilantro, and a squeeze of lime.

Step 7: Serve hot and enjoy your delicious grilled tofu tacos!

Helpful Tips:
1. Marinate tofu in a mixture of soy sauce, lime juice, and garlic before grilling for maximum flavor.

2. Use firm or extra firm tofu to ensure it holds its shape during grilling.

3. Make a spicy mayo or avocado crema to drizzle over the tacos for added creaminess.

4. Grill the tofu on high heat for a crispy exterior and smoky flavor.

5. Fill the tacos with grilled tofu, fresh veggies, and a sprinkle of cilantro for a healthy and delicious meal. Enjoy!

Lemon garlic shrimp skewers

Ingredients:
- 1 lb large shrimp
- 2 lemons
- 5 cloves garlic
- 1/4 cup olive oil
- Salt and pepper
- Fresh parsley (optional)

Equipment:
1. Skewers
2. Mixing bowl
3. Whisk
4. Knife
5. Cutting board

Methods:
Step 1: Start by marinating the shrimp in a mixture of lemon juice, minced garlic, olive oil, salt, and pepper for at least 30 minutes.

Step 2: Thread the marinated shrimp onto skewers, alternating with slices of lemon and chunks of red onion.

Step 3: Preheat your grill to medium-high heat and lightly oil the grates to prevent sticking.

Step 4: Place the shrimp skewers on the grill and cook for 2-3 minutes per side, or until they are pink and opaque.

Step 5: Remove the skewers from the grill and serve hot with additional lemon wedges for squeezing. Enjoy your delicious lemon garlic shrimp skewers!

Helpful Tips:
1. Marinate the shrimp in lemon juice, minced garlic, olive oil, salt, and pepper for at least 30 minutes.

2. Soak wooden skewers in water for at least 30 minutes to prevent burning while grilling.

3. Assemble shrimp onto skewers, leaving some space between each piece for even cooking.

4. Preheat grill to medium-high heat and lightly oil the grates to prevent sticking.

5. Grill skewers for 2-3 minutes per side, until shrimp are opaque and slightly charred.

6. Serve with additional lemon slices and garnish with chopped parsley for extra flavor. Enjoy!

Cauliflower and broccoli curry

Ingredients:

- 1 head cauliflower
- 1 head broccoli
- 1 can coconut milk
- 1 onion
- 2 garlic cloves
- 1 tbsp curry powder
- 1 tsp turmeric
- 1/2 tsp cayenne pepper
- Salt to taste

Equipment:

1. Knife
2. Cutting board
3. Saucepan
4. Wooden spoon
5. Strainer
6. Fry pan

Methods:

Step 1: Wash and chop 1 head of cauliflower and 1 head of broccoli into florets.

Step 2: Heat 2 tablespoons of oil in a large pan over medium heat.

Step 3: Add 1 diced onion and cook until translucent.

Step 4: Mix in 2 minced garlic cloves, 1 tablespoon of curry powder, 1 teaspoon of turmeric, and 1 teaspoon of cumin.

Step 5: Add the cauliflower and broccoli florets to the pan and stir to coat in the spices.

Step 6: Pour in 1 can of coconut milk and bring to a simmer.

Step 7: Cover and cook for 15-20 minutes, or until the vegetables are tender.

Step 8: Serve the curry over rice or with naan bread. Enjoy!

Helpful Tips:

1. Start by washing and chopping the cauliflower and broccoli into bite-sized florets.

2. Heat oil in a pan and add in cumin seeds, mustard seeds, and curry leaves for added flavor.

3. Sauté onions, garlic, and ginger until golden brown before adding in a mixture of turmeric, cumin, coriander, and garam masala for seasoning.

4. Add in the cauliflower and broccoli florets, along with some water, and simmer until the veggies are tender.

5. Finish off with a splash of coconut milk for creaminess and garnish with fresh cilantro before serving over rice or with naan bread. Enjoy!

Baked chicken and vegetable casserole

Ingredients:

- 4 chicken breasts
- 2 cups of mixed vegetables
- 1 cup of chicken broth
- 1/2 cup of grated cheese

Equipment:

1. Baking dish
2. Mixing bowl
3. Knife
4. Cutting board
5. Baking sheet

Methods:

Step 1: Preheat the oven to 375°F.

Step 2: Season chicken breasts with salt, pepper, and Italian seasoning.

Step 3: Place the seasoned chicken in a baking dish.

Step 4: Add chopped vegetables such as bell peppers, onions, and zucchini around the chicken.

Step 5: Drizzle olive oil over the chicken and vegetables.

Step 6: Cover the baking dish with foil and bake for 30 minutes.

Step 7: Remove foil and bake for an additional 15-20 minutes or until chicken is cooked through.

Step 8: Sprinkle with grated Parmesan cheese and broil for 2-3 minutes.

Step 9: Serve hot and enjoy your delicious baked chicken and vegetable casserole.

Helpful Tips:

1. Preheat your oven to the appropriate temperature, usually around 375 degrees Fahrenheit.

2. Season your chicken with salt, pepper, and any other desired seasonings before placing it in the casserole dish.

3. Cut your vegetables into similar size pieces to ensure even cooking.

4. Layer the vegetables on the bottom of the casserole dish to create a bed for the chicken to sit on.

5. Add a bit of chicken broth or water to the dish to help keep the chicken moist during cooking.

6. Cover the casserole dish with foil before baking to lock in moisture.

7. Check the chicken for doneness by using a meat thermometer - it should reach 165 degrees Fahrenheit.

8. Finish by broiling the dish for a few minutes to crisp up the chicken skin. Enjoy!

Black bean and corn salad

Ingredients:
- 1 can black beans (15 oz)
- 1 cup corn kernels
- 1/2 red bell pepper, diced
- 1/4 cup red onion, chopped
- 1/4 cup cilantro, chopped

Equipment:
1. Knife
2. Cutting board
3. Mixing bowl
4. Wooden spoon
5. Serving platter

Methods:
Step 1: Rinse 1 can of black beans and 1 cup of corn in a colander under cold water.

Step 2: In a large mixing bowl, combine the rinsed black beans and corn.

Step 3: Add 1 diced red bell pepper, 1 diced avocado, and 1/4 cup of chopped cilantro to the bowl.

Step 4: In a small bowl, whisk together 1/4 cup of olive oil, 2 tablespoons of lime juice, 1 teaspoon of cumin, salt, and pepper.

Step 5: Pour the dressing over the black bean and corn mixture and toss to combine.

Step 6: Serve chilled and enjoy!

Helpful Tips:
1. Start by rinsing and draining a can of black beans and a can of sweet corn.
2. Mix the black beans and corn in a large bowl.
3. Add diced red bell pepper, red onion, and fresh cilantro to the mixture for added flavor.
4. Dress the salad with a mix of olive oil, lime juice, cumin, salt, and pepper.
5. Toss everything together gently to combine all the flavors.

6. Let the salad sit in the fridge for at least 30 minutes to allow the flavors to meld together.

7. Serve chilled as a side dish or over a bed of lettuce for a light meal.

Turkey and vegetable curry

Ingredients:

- 500g turkey breast
- 2 cups mixed vegetables
- 1 onion, chopped
- 2 garlic cloves, minced
- 1 can coconut milk
- 2 tbsp curry powder
- Salt, pepper to taste

Equipment:

1. Saucepan
2. Cooking spoon
3. Chef's knife
4. Cutting board
5. Skillet

Methods:

Step 1: Heat oil in a large pot over medium heat.

Step 2: Add chopped onions and garlic, cook until softened.

Step 3: Stir in chopped turkey breast and brown on all sides.

Step 4: Add curry powder, cumin, coriander, and turmeric, cook for 1 minute.

Step 5: Pour in coconut milk and chicken broth, bring to a simmer.

Step 6: Add chopped vegetables such as carrots, potatoes, and bell peppers.

Step 7: Cover the pot and let the curry simmer for 20-25 minutes, stirring occasionally.

Step 8: Serve hot over rice or with naan bread. Enjoy your delicious turkey and vegetable curry!

Helpful Tips:

1. Brown the turkey meat before adding it to the curry for extra flavor.
2. Use a mix of seasonal vegetables for added freshness and nutrients.

3. Toast whole spices like cumin, coriander, and mustard seeds before grinding for a more intense flavor.

4. Add a bit of yogurt or coconut milk to the curry for a creamy texture.

5. Taste and adjust seasonings before serving, adding more salt, pepper, or spices as needed.

Lentil and vegetable pasta

Ingredients:

- 1 cup of lentils
- 8 oz of pasta
- 2 carrots, diced
- 1 onion, diced
- 1 can of diced tomatoes
- 4 cups of vegetable broth
- 2 cloves of garlic, minced

Equipment:

1. Pot
2. Strainer
3. Knife
4. Cutting board
5. Saute pan
6. Wooden spoon

Methods:

Step 1: Boil a pot of water and cook pasta according to package instructions.

Step 2: In a separate pan, heat olive oil and sauté chopped onion and minced garlic.

Step 3: Add diced carrots, bell peppers, and zucchini to the pan and cook until softened.

Step 4: Stir in cooked lentils, diced tomatoes, and vegetable broth.

Step 5: Season with salt, pepper, and dried herbs like basil and oregano.

Step 6: Let the mixture simmer for 10-15 minutes until flavors are well combined.

Step 7: Serve the lentil and vegetable sauce over the cooked pasta.

Step 8: Enjoy your delicious Lentil and vegetable pasta dish!

Helpful Tips:

BRINTALOS GEORGIOS

1. Start by cooking your pasta according to package instructions while you prepare your vegetables.

2. Heat olive oil in a pan and sauté diced onions, bell peppers, and zucchini until caramelized.

3. Add minced garlic and cook for another minute.

4. Stir in cooked lentils and your favorite pasta sauce, simmering until heated through.

5. Season with salt, pepper, and a pinch of red pepper flakes for some heat.

6. Serve the vegetable and lentil sauce over the cooked pasta, garnishing with fresh basil or parsley.

7. Enjoy a nutritious and delicious Lentil and Vegetable Pasta dish!

Grilled portobello mushroom burger

Ingredients:
- 4 portobello mushrooms
- 4 burger buns
- 1 red onion, sliced
- 1 red bell pepper, sliced
- 4 slices of Swiss cheese

Equipment:
1. Grill pan
2. Spatula
3. Knife
4. Cutting board
5. Mixing bowl

Methods:
Step 1: Preheat the grill to medium-high heat.

Step 2: Clean the portobello mushrooms and remove the stems.

Step 3: In a small bowl, mix together olive oil, balsamic vinegar, minced garlic, salt, and pepper.

Step 4: Brush the mushroom caps with the olive oil mixture.

Step 5: Place the mushrooms on the grill and cook for 4-5 minutes on each side.

Step 6: Toast the burger buns on the grill.

Step 7: Assemble the burger by placing the grilled mushroom on the bottom bun.

Step 8: Add your favorite toppings like lettuce, tomato, avocado, and cheese.

Step 9: Top with the remaining bun and enjoy!

Helpful Tips:
1. Clean the portobello mushrooms thoroughly, removing any dirt or debris from the caps.

2. Remove the stems of the mushrooms to create a flat surface for grilling.

3. Marinate the mushrooms in a mixture of olive oil, balsamic vinegar, garlic, and herbs for at least 30 minutes before grilling.

4. Preheat your grill to medium-high heat and oil the grates to prevent sticking.

5. Grill the portobello mushrooms for 4-5 minutes on each side, or until they are tender and have nice grill marks.

6. Serve the grilled portobello mushrooms on toasted burger buns with your favorite toppings like lettuce, tomato, avocado, and cheese. Enjoy your delicious vegetarian burger!

Lemon dill baked salmon

Ingredients:

- 4 salmon fillets (6 oz each)
- 2 tbsp olive oil
- 2 tbsp lemon juice
- 2 cloves garlic, minced
- 2 tsp dried dill
- Salt and pepper to taste

Equipment:

1. Baking Dish
2. Mixing Bowl
3. Basting Brush
4. Aluminum Foil (optional)
5. Oven Mitts
6. Serving Platter

Methods:

Step 1: Preheat the oven to 375°F.

Step 2: In a small bowl, mix together 1/4 cup of olive oil, 2 tablespoons of lemon juice, and 2 tablespoons of chopped dill.

Step 3: Place the salmon fillets on a baking sheet lined with parchment paper.

Step 4: Brush the lemon dill mixture onto the salmon fillets.

Step 5: Season the salmon with salt and pepper to taste.

Step 6: Bake the salmon in the preheated oven for 15-20 minutes, or until it is cooked through and flakes easily with a fork.

Step 7: Serve the lemon dill baked salmon hot and enjoy!

Helpful Tips:

1. Preheat the oven to 400°F and line a baking dish with parchment paper.

2. Rub the salmon fillets with olive oil and season with salt and pepper.

3. In a small bowl, mix together chopped dill, minced garlic, lemon zest, and lemon juice.

4. Spread the dill mixture over the salmon fillets.

5. Bake the salmon for 12-15 minutes, or until it flakes easily with a fork.

6. Serve the lemon dill baked salmon with a side of roasted vegetables or a fresh salad.

7. Don't overcook the salmon to keep it juicy and flavorful.

Grilled chicken breast with steamed vegetables

Ingredients:

- 4 chicken breasts
- 2 cups mixed vegetables
- Olive oil
- Salt
- Pepper

Equipment:

1. Grill pan
2. Steamer basket
3. Tongs
4. Cooking spatula
5. Knife
6. Cutting board

Methods:

Step 1: Preheat grill to medium-high heat.

Step 2: Season chicken breast with salt, pepper, and any desired herbs or spices.

Step 3: Place chicken breast on grill and cook for 6-7 minutes per side, or until internal temperature reaches 165°F.

Step 4: While chicken is cooking, steam vegetables such as broccoli, carrots, and bell peppers.

Step 5: After chicken is cooked, let it rest for a few minutes before slicing.

Step 6: Serve grilled chicken breast with steamed vegetables on the side.

Step 7: Enjoy your delicious and healthy meal!

Helpful Tips:

1. Preheat your grill to medium-high heat before adding your chicken breast.

2. Season the chicken breast with your favorite spices and marinate for at least 30 minutes.

3. Grill the chicken for about 6-7 minutes on each side or until the internal temperature reaches 165°F.

4. For steaming vegetables, place them in a steamer basket over a pot of boiling water for about 5-7 minutes until tender-crisp.

5. Season the vegetables with salt, pepper, and a drizzle of olive oil for added flavor.

6. Serve the grilled chicken breast with the steamed vegetables for a healthy and delicious meal.

Baked cod with lemon and herbs

Ingredients:

- 4 cod fillets
- 1 lemon
- 2 tbsp olive oil
- 1 garlic clove
- 1 tbsp fresh herbs
- Salt and pepper to taste

Equipment:

1. Baking dish
2. Mixing bowl
3. Whisk
4. Tongs
5. Baking sheet

Methods:

Step 1: Preheat the oven to 400°F and line a baking dish with parchment paper.

Step 2: Rinse the cod fillets under cold water and pat them dry with paper towels.

Step 3: Place the cod fillets in the prepared baking dish.

Step 4: Drizzle the cod fillets with olive oil and squeeze fresh lemon juice over them.

Step 5: Sprinkle the cod fillets with chopped herbs such as parsley, dill, and thyme.

Step 6: Season the cod fillets with salt and pepper.

Step 7: Bake the cod fillets in the preheated oven for 15-20 minutes, or until they are cooked through and flake easily with a fork.

Step 8: Serve the baked cod with additional lemon wedges, if desired. Enjoy!

Helpful Tips:

BRINTALOS GEORGIOS

1. Preheat your oven to 400°F and line a baking sheet with parchment paper.

2. Season the cod fillets with salt, pepper, and any herbs of your choice (such as parsley, thyme, or rosemary).

3. Place the seasoned cod on the prepared baking sheet and drizzle with olive oil and lemon juice.

4. Bake the cod in the preheated oven for 12-15 minutes, or until it is opaque and flakes easily with a fork.

5. Garnish with additional lemon slices and fresh herbs before serving. Enjoy your delicious baked cod with lemon and herbs!

Turkey chili with mixed beans

Ingredients:
- 1 lb ground turkey
- 1 can of black beans (15 oz)
- 1 can of kidney beans (15 oz)
- 1 can of diced tomatoes (14.5 oz)
- 1 onion, chopped
- 1 bell pepper, chopped
- 2 cloves of garlic, minced
- 1 tbsp chili powder
- 1 tsp cumin
- Salt and pepper to taste

Equipment:
1. Large pot
2. Wooden spoon
3. Knife
4. Cutting board
5. Can opener

Methods:
Step 1: Heat olive oil in a large pot over medium heat.

Step 2: Add chopped onions and cook until softened, about 5 minutes.

Step 3: Stir in minced garlic and cook for another minute.

Step 4: Add ground turkey and cook until browned, breaking it up with a spoon.

Step 5: Stir in chili powder, cumin, paprika, and salt.

Step 6: Pour in diced tomatoes, tomato sauce, and chicken broth.

Step 7: Add mixed beans and stir to combine.

Step 8: Bring the chili to a simmer and let it cook for 20-30 minutes.

Step 9: Serve hot with toppings like shredded cheese, sour cream, and chopped cilantro.

Helpful Tips:

BRINTALOS GEORGIOS

1. Start by browning ground turkey in a large pot over medium-high heat.

2. Add diced onions, garlic, and bell peppers to the pot and cook until softened.

3. Stir in diced tomatoes, tomato sauce, and chicken broth for a flavorful base.

4. Season with chili powder, cumin, and a pinch of cayenne for heat.

5. Drain and rinse a variety of canned beans (such as kidney, black, and pinto) before adding them to the pot.

6. Let the chili simmer for at least 30 minutes to allow flavors to meld together.

7. Serve hot with shredded cheese, sour cream, and diced avocado for toppings. Enjoy!

Quinoa salad with vegetables and vinaigrette

Ingredients:

- 1 cup quinoa
- 1 red bell pepper, chopped
- 1 cucumber, diced
- 1/2 red onion, finely sliced
- 1/4 cup olive oil
- 2 tbsp balsamic vinegar
- 1 tsp Dijon mustard
- Salt and pepper to taste

Equipment:

1. Mixing bowl
2. Whisk
3. Cutting board
4. Knife
5. Saucepan
6. Salad bowl

Methods:

Step 1: Rinse 1 cup of quinoa in a fine mesh strainer under running water.

Step 2: In a medium saucepan, bring 2 cups of water to a boil.

Step 3: Add the quinoa, reduce heat to low, cover, and simmer for 15 minutes.

Step 4: Remove from heat and let it sit for 5 minutes. Fluff with a fork.

Step 5: In a large bowl, combine cooked quinoa with chopped vegetables like bell peppers, cucumbers, and cherry tomatoes.

Step 6: In a small bowl, whisk together olive oil, lemon juice, and honey for the vinaigrette.

Step 7: Pour the vinaigrette over the salad and toss to combine. Enjoy!

Helpful Tips:

1. Cook quinoa according to package instructions for best results.

2. Chop a variety of colorful vegetables like bell peppers, cucumbers, and cherry tomatoes for added flavor and texture.

3. Prepare a simple vinaigrette dressing with olive oil, lemon juice, Dijon mustard, and honey.

4. Mix the cooked quinoa and chopped vegetables together in a large bowl.

5. Drizzle the vinaigrette over the salad and toss to combine.

6. Season with salt and pepper to taste.

7. Serve chilled or at room temperature for a refreshing and nutritious meal.

Milton Keynes UK
Ingram Content Group UK Ltd.
UKHW020738010424
440421UK00014B/882